Sade—
Be you.
You R.
A future you're watching
I'm watching
[signature]

THE WORLD CHANGER'S
GUIDE

Laura Hudson

Copyright © 2017 Laura Hudson
All rights reserved.
ISBN-13: 978-1545410875

DEDICATIONS

Dad, Mom, Lisa and Benny
Thank you for making life worth living and never letting me believe otherwise.

Cross, Chaz and Lyv
You are the loves of my life. Thank you for never thinking it was weird that your Mom didn't have hair. You always thought it was weird that everyone else's did.

Denise
I could thank you in one million books and it still wouldn't be enough.

Tera
Thank you for making me look so good on the cover. I'm only as good as the company I keep and I am good!

Anthony Carrigan
I am still amazed that you would take time out of your crazy, busy life to read my book - much less write a foreword. I am forever grateful. I love you too!

My Alopecia Community
I love you all! My story is your story. Let's spread the word and change the world with unicorn love.

Betsy Woytovich

The best editor ever! Just when I think you can't impact my life any more than you already have – you go and do this!

The Red Horse Inn & Stone Soup Restaurant - Landrum, SC

Thank you for letting me sit in your beautiful establishments and get away from life long enough to finish my book. I promise I'll be back soon!

CONTENTS:

DEDICATIONS 4

FOREWORD 8

INTRODUCTION 12

ACKNOWLEDGEMENTS...15

DREAMER 17

STRUGGLE 23

VICTIMS 28

DADDY 34

NOTICED 45

CAN'T 53

MOVES 73

ADJUSTED 83

OUT...93

BELONGING 102

PEOPLE..110

FREE 117

LOVED 126

CURSED 133

ENOUGH...139

ABOUT THE AUTHOR 144

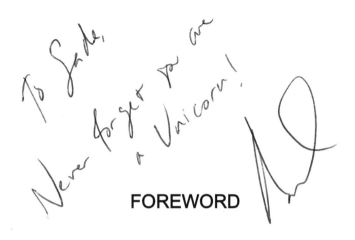

To Jade,
Never forget to are a Unicorn!

FOREWORD

by Anthony Carrigan

Hey readers, what's up?! I'm Anthony, actor, alopecian, alliterationist. Hi! So first off I want to commend you for picking up this book. You have chosen wisely.

I mean I'm biased since me and Laura are really good pals. So good in fact, that I had to scrap the first draft of this foreword because my friends who read it asked me with deep concern, "dude...are you in love with Laura Hudson?"

Short answer, yes, but it's a unicorn love. I'll explain.

I've always said that growing up with alopecia was like being a lone unicorn: solitary, strange, somehow different from the herd and therefore unable to recognize my own beauty. My journey to discovering how beautiful and magical being a unicorn is-was a difficult one; especially as an actor in an image centered business. Once I did embrace my alopecia unicorn-ness the world opened up. It changed.

All of the sudden I was a totally hairless actor and changing the rules of the business with each step. Before I knew it, this lone unicorn was speaking at a freaking unicorn convention (aka Children's Alopecia Project's Alopeciapalooza) and I could see all of these beautiful bald faces mirroring what I could never see growing up. It took so many years to get there.

All of those years I wished, wished so hard for something like this book.

While reading Laura's book, there were dozens of times when I would say (or yell) out loud "I know what that feels like!" or "Totally" or "I TOTALLY KNOW WHAT THAT FEELS LIKE." Her conversational tone has the warmth and ease of a dear friend over a cup of tea at a kitchen table.

These stories, so delicately woven with rich detail will make you thankful that there are friends along the way that will do anything for you, that help can come from the most unexpected places, and that the times of the hardest suffering yield the greatest lessons. You don't need to be an alopecian in order to get something from this book. Everyone can relate to this in some deep and meaningful way. Regardless of what bag of rocks you've been carrying, this is a manual for turning those rocks to gemstones. Keep reading. Trust me.

The secrets of changing the world are at your fingertips. Or unicorn hooves.

Enjoy.

INTRODUCTION

I'm a world changer. With no athletic ability or true fame to attribute it to, one day, I decided to be okay with my skin and to be someone who lit up the room when I entered and left an impression upon my exit.

I am the kid who is picked on in school to the point of wanting to die. I am the rejected girl with no date to the prom. I am the sick patient with no cure. I am the heartbroken girl that just wants to be loved. I am the high school dropout that has a higher statistical chance at being unemployed than successful. I am destined to be all of these things.

I am determined to be none of these things.

That's the thing about being a world changer, you
have to be willing to leave something behind. I chose to shed the bad and rise up with all that was good. This is my guide for taking an ordinary human being and turning that person into someone worth writing about.

ACKNOWLEDGEMENTS

This book is dedicated to...

everyone that was ever told they wouldn't
amount to anything
anyone who has ever cried him- or herself to
sleep
the unloved
the unwanted
the dreamers with no hope of success
sons and daughters who will never live up to
their parents' expectations
high school dropouts
college failures
lost souls in search of an answer
the sick and dying
the lonely hearts
the bullied and rejected
those who do not fit the mold of normal
the freaks
the monsters
you
me

DREAMER

I am a dreamer. I always have been. I blame my parents really. They never told me that there was anything that I couldn't do. Maybe I talked too much and they were just nodding their heads not really listening, but if I could dream it, they made me think I could do it.

This encouragement continued throughout my school years. In my book you'll read instances of heartbreak and torment from being picked on as a child. There are also many moments of people who were placed in my path to teach me to stand confident and even run towards greatness. Those people may have possibly created a monster.

I found a paper from school where I had been asked to fill in the blank to, "When I grow up, I want to be _____," and I had written in **Famous**.

You'd think at 40 years old, I would look back at that and find it immature or ridiculous, but I don't. If you asked me the same question today, I'd give you the very same answer.

I am a dreamer and I dream of travelling the world. I imagine myself meeting people from all facets of life from homeless street performers to Queens (both the demographic & the royalty). I see my family gathering around the television to watch me on a Late Night TV Show appearance.

I am a dreamer.

There is nothing that I can think of that I do not believe I could do. Call me arrogant or delusional, but it's the truth. Absolutely anything you can do, I can do and possibly do better. Well, at least I'll break an arm trying.

I remember when I was a little girl, Mattel had a Barbie commercial out where these little girls sang the song, "We girls can do anything – right Barbie?" I would sing that song in everything I did! Funny enough, I sing it occasionally now just to make myself laugh.

I can do anything.

It's this dreamer attitude that has gotten me through some really hard times. It's this dreamer mentality that has given me vision through the nightmares.

My dream of more is what has forced me to stand up, brush myself off and keep moving forward.

My children have inherited this from me and it is a legacy of purpose that I am proud to watch them carry. We are happy. We are fulfilled. We are making the most out of what we have been given while pressing forward to the next level in life.

Yes, I am a dreamer, but I've worked hard to turn my dreams into reality. Today, as I am sitting in the gathering room of The Red Horse Inn in Landrum, SC, facing a breathtaking mountain view, writing in an all white room – I dream of a finished book. Once that dream comes true, my next dream is for it to be published and then I dream of you reading it.

See, that's not so arrogant right?

Let's talk about the real purpose behind this book. I have a unique story. A few times each year, I travel to different parts of the country telling my story. I have Alopecia Universalis, an autoimmune disease for which there is no cure. My body does not grow hair. I live my life as a bald woman and, as you can imagine, I stand out quite a bit in the world of hairy people.

Sometimes I'm bold and a bit cocky about being different, and sometimes I secretly wish I had a head of beautiful hair. More times than not, I wish I had a purple mohawk. Knowing this, makes it not seem as unbelievable that I am comfortable being bald.

I've been amazed throughout the years at how many relatable experiences my story has presented to me. I meet someone everyday who stops to talk to me about being bald. Sometimes it is because they assume I have cancer and other times, they want to tell me they think I am brave or inspiring. I've heard so many stories over the years of hurt and heartbreak from loss. I remind them of their sister who died from breast cancer and they just want a hug. I hug them while they cry.

Usually, they stop me to tell me that I am beautiful.

What a gift! A gift that I do not take for granted.

Almost daily, a stranger tells me I am beautiful. So many women go their whole life without hearing this. So many confidence and emotional issues are born in girls from simply not being told they are beautiful.

I know people only stop me because they are amazed that I am bald and look so healthy and they want to know why. I know that some people only tell me I am beautiful because they think I am dying of cancer and they want to make me feel better. Regardless of the reason, I'll take it. A woman can never receive too many compliments.

Before I get into the funny stories and tear jerking moments, I want to explain the purpose of this book. This is more than just my life story. This is my life story told in a way that I hope encourages you to be a world changer.

I'm more than a dreamer. I don't just dream about caviar and limo rides. I don't just dream about fame and fortune. I dream of something bigger. I want to change the world, my world and your world.

Tag along with me through this compilation of stories and learn in each instance how you can relate it to your own story. Learn how your life struggles can impact the struggles of those around you.

Before you can really become a world changer, we need to talk about something that really bothers me. I'd like to take a moment to define struggle. Shall we?

STRUGGLE

We all define struggle differently. The definition of struggle ranges from a bad haircut to having no food to feed your family. Although some struggles are more significant, they are equally heavy at the moment.

As you read through this book, my story, you will find yourself comparing your struggles to mine. You may discount some of my hurt and think I have no idea what it really means to struggle. On the flip side, you may feel as if you are a total wimp complaining about your petty problems compared to what I've been through.

To both of you, I say, "Look beyond yourself!" Seriously, look beyond your own circumstances and put yourself in my shoes. That is a great lesson to learn in life. That's the first lesson of this book.

Empathy: the ability to understand and share the feelings of another.

No two stories are alike. You are never going to find someone that you can relate to on a complete level. We are literally living in a "choose your own adventure" storybook life where we may start off on the same path together, but at some point we will take a different turn.

Rather than comparing your story to mine, make the effort to understand and share in my struggles. Try to find ways that you can identify with me and learn from my journey. If you carry this habit outside of reading my words and into life, your worldview will change. The ability to recognize your struggles in someone else's is power. The student becomes the teacher, and the world becomes your classroom.

Empathy is not turning the conversation back to you and is not meant to plunge you deeper into your own depths of self-loathing. You do not have permission to take on the burden of others or to hand your burdens to an unsuspecting victim.

Empathy is recognizing that the woman who is crying herself to sleep over a cheating spouse needs to know that you once went through something similar when you lost your mother and grieved over the loss. This goes against everything we are taught to feel.

As a society, we take offense to someone thinking that their pain is as great as our pain. We dare you to say "I understand," if you've never been through exactly what we are going through. Our skin is so thin that we've lost the ability to offer empathy to another who we have judged and deemed less hurt.

Have you ever had a car repossessed? How did it feel in that moment? It feels desperate, hopeless and as if you can't face the future of losing anything else. You just want to cry and puke at that same time.

Now think about what it feels like to have lost a precious family heirloom. It is sickening and a reminder that you will never have it to hand down to your own child. You just want to cry and puke at the same time.

How does it feel to lose a loved one? It's devastating and often crippling. I imagine you cry and feel like you are going to puke at the same time.

There's a common denominator to all three scenarios. Each instance is overwhelming to the point that you don't know if you are going to cry or puke. Imagine if we could identify with others in a way that we didn't weigh our struggles but rather considered the hurt as equally devastating in that moment of that person's life.

An empathetic society is one that seeks to understand the struggle of another and is willing to find a way to relate to this person so that their own strength might bring hope.

It's not easy.

When you are facing something so painful and someone tries to compare their petty, small personal experience to yours, it is natural to feel resentful. You will want to either put them in their place or secretly hold it against them. Don't do it! Rather, use the moment to relate and learn.

Start with my story. As it unfolds through the chapters of this book, relate to me. Learn from me. As I become stronger through my struggles, you will find ways to condition your own life and hopefully come out at the end of this book stronger. Learn from my mistakes, pain and triumphs.

Consider my story your story. We are in this thing together. Look at you showing empathy. It looks so good on you.

VICTIMS

I started out as a pretty normal kid. My Mom claims I never pitched fits or misbehaved, but she also claimed her water never broke during labor, so I'm not buying either story. It was the late 70's, early 80's, and I cannot think back on a single insecurity that I might have possessed.

I can remember going to play with the neighborhood kids, learning my ABC's and listening to books on tape using the little headphones and player in the school library. During this time, I have no memories of any form of bullying or ever thinking of myself as different.

I do remember my Kindergarten teacher pinching me on St. Patrick's Day because I was not wearing any green. It was 1980, and they still paddled and pinched for that matter. After she pinched me, I got so embarrassed that I asked to go to the restroom. Lo and behold, I realized in the bathroom that I had worn green underwear that day! I immediately ran out to the class and announced that I had on green underwear. She totally took back that pinch.

This story has very little relevance to my journey other than to prove what I will mention in the book about me being competitive and needing to prove when I am right. There's something psychological behind both I'm sure. I'll let you be the judge of that.

I remember being sick sometimes and having to go to the hospital. Once I had to stay in an oxygen tent because of a bout of pneumonia. My parents had requested prayer for me saying I was hospitalized. I went back to church and argued that I had "gone camping." I haven't changed much.

I had asthma and seizures, but I have no traumatic memories of either. My brother and sister, however, do possibly have PTSD as a result of two of my seizures.

In one instance, I was about 10 months old. My sister Lisa was ten years old, and my brother Benny, six years old. I was having a seizure, and my Mom told Lisa to hold me on her lap in the backseat and, "don't let her swallow her tongue." To hear my sister tell this story, she was rightfully terrified!

Mom drove to the police station because someone told her that doing so would prompt emergency help. She didn't have a phone, so calling 911 wasn't an option. After leaving for the hospital with me in an ambulance, they realized that she had parked in front of the station's gas tanks, and the cops couldn't fill up their cars. Crime went scott free that day I guess.

Another seizure incident remains in the family tales and is often told when we are all together. I'll start with the car. My parents had a Dodge Charger (yes, just like the Dukes of Hazzard car) and my Dad drove that thing down the road like a bat out of Hell. He was in such a hurry that he almost left Mom who was running me to the car. In fact, he drove so fast and with so much punch, the hospital staff heard him coming and had a gurney ready and waiting.

Let me add, this was in the middle of the night, and my family didn't have the best pajama situation happening. Mom's bra was holding on by one hook. Lisa had on a halter top and flannel pants rolled up as high as she could roll them. Benny was wearing a Hulk t-shirt and underwear with holes in them. They are half dressed, in the back seat of a car being driven by a maniac, holding a seizing toddler, all while hoping she doesn't swallow her tongue.

They arrived at the hospital and my parents told my siblings to stay in the car and wait. Again, this is the late 70's and they didn't make the wisest decisions, but we lived. As Lisa and Benny waited in the car, the car started smoking and making a strange popping noise. Benny, 8, turned to Lisa, 12, and exclaimed, "It's going to explode!" They did what any rational half-dressed children would do in that situation and they fled the vehicle to seek safe ground in the hospital.

As you can imagine, these poor homeless orphans ran into the hospital frantically fleeing the scene of a potential massive explosion. The staff felt so sorry for them that they fed them and gave them clothes to wear. As much as I would like to say I was the victim in this situation, having had a grand mal seizure, I must give all victim rights to my sister and brother.

See, you would rationally think the biggest victim was the child having the seizure, but I was basically unconscious. I have no recollection of that night whatsoever.

Think for a moment about the two young children who were very present though thinking their sister could die, and that it could be their fault if she died from swallowing her tongue, not to mention the fear that they too almost died, burned alive in their vehicle. Although their trauma is completely irrational (I couldn't swallow my tongue, it wasn't their fault, and the car was merely cooling off), their struggle was real.

Now 37 years later, they still talk about it. Granted we laugh quite a bit about it, but the fear is remembered.

That's the thing about struggles. It is so easy to look at the obvious victims and ignore the ones that played a small role. I think about my siblings' night of terror and I am reminded of those that I know who suffer from anxiety disorders. It has been a reminder to realize that the moment is very real to that person and to not discount the panic that it brings.

DADDY

It started so small for me. I fell and hit my head when I was 18 months old. Well, I later found out that my sister dropped me, but who's keeping score? Me, I'm keeping score. This fact served me well when I needed some leverage in sibling negotiations.

I ended up with a goose-egg-sized bump on my head, but the doctors were not concerned. My parents were assured at this time that, "It will go away. Everything is normal." The bump on my head did go away, but the hair where the bump was went away as well. I was left with a goose-egg-sized bald spot. I was diagnosed as a toddler with Alopecia Areata. Alopecia Areata is just like it sounds – bald in areas.

My Mom's main memory from my diagnosis day is "I cried all the way home." She would call her Mom and together they would cry it out. I would learn many years later; they weren't the only ones who cried.

My sister was and still is beautiful. As a teenager, she had Farrah Fawcett hair. That was a big deal in the late 70's, early 80's, I suppose. We were born 10 years apart.

In the mornings, as she was fixing her hair for school, I would sit on the countertop and watch her get ready. I would stare in awe and fascination as she feathered and sprayed her hair. I would pretend to fix my own hair as she fixed hers. In my little girl innocence, I broke her heart when I would say, "I wish I had hair like you." It bothered her so much that she started locking the door to the bathroom when she got ready. Otherwise, I'd make her start her days in tears.

I had a little hair. It was thin and had noticeable bald spots, but my Mom got creative. She would part it on one side and use a barrette to hide the slick skin showing through. From doctors to hair stylists, my Mom was given some pretty crazy advice at this point.

She heard "wisdom" such as:

1. Don't let her look in a mirror.

If she sees the bald spots, it'll be too traumatizing.

So I didn't look at the back of my head in the mirror. My Mom fixed my hair for me. I have a memory of being about eight or nine, before the wig, of my Mom trying to figure out how to fix my hair strategically. I was so confused.

2. She could die.

I was two years old and the doctors had no idea why my blood work was so wonky and my hair was falling out. They advised my parents to keep their travel plans and take me to Disney World. Make some memories; they may be her last. To quote, "Let her have the time of her life."

Although I didn't know what it meant, this was my first instance of Alopecia Perks. An Alopecia perk is an occasion where a person with alopecia receives something for free or special treatment because the giver assumes he or she is either dying or sick.

Most Alopecians are aware of this occurrence and have benefited from it in some way. For me, I got to go to Disney World at 2 years old.

3. Stress causes Alopecia. She must be stressed.

At 18 months old, I was apparently so stressed that I had given myself an autoimmune disorder. I sure hope that sounds as ridiculous to you as it does to me.

The sad part is that they still use this cause today. They tell newly diagnosed Alopecians that the cause is stress. I'm screaming at the top of my lungs with this one, "STOP BLAMING STRESS FOR THIS AUTOIMMUNE DISORDER!"

There, I feel better.

4. It's like when you skin your knee - it'll grow back.

Seriously, my Mom was told this from well-meaning people. For the record, NEVER say this to someone with Alopecia, in any context. Hair does not always grow back. A lizard can regrow a leg, do you tell an amputee, "it might grow back"? No! That would make you an idiot.

Point made? I'm moving on.

5. Get used to having a bald headed kid.

My parents were given this awesome piece of medical advice at one point. They both describe not knowing what to do with this information. What does having a bald kid mean exactly? There's no instruction manual for taking care of a "bald kid." This statement created insecurities of what I may or may not have to face for the rest of my life. Perhaps this is where the "cover it up with a wig" idea was born.

6. It was the sins of the parents that caused it.

My Father was actually accused of causing my health condition because he had "sin" in his life. This sin was that when he was younger he maybe smoked cigarettes and drank beer. That was an unfair burden for him to have to carry. I can't even begin to imagine the impact the lie must have had on his confidence as a father.

It's bad enough that his daughter is sick and he can't do anything about it, but now he has insensitive, ugly people telling him it is his fault.

If you are reading this book and you told my father that my Alopecia was a result of sin in his life, yes, I just called you insensitive and ugly. You should call him and apologize.

We had zero support, no one to relate to. I was the only person on the planet with Alopecia as far as we were concerned. There was an "organization" for people with Alopecia, but they really didn't offer us any support. I was nine years old with a condition about which I was uneducated, misinformed and isolated, and the only mail I ever received from them was donation pleas. It got to the point that I didn't even open the mail I received from the organization. In 30 years, their message is still the same, "give us money for research so we can find a cure."

Again, we had no support, no roadmap to follow and my hair was falling out. It was in the middle of a Tennessee winter and I was cold. My Mom tried to help the situation by making me wear a hat. A knit hat to be exact. If you are from the South in the United States, it is called a Toboggan. I would take it off and leave it wherever I wanted. On the floor, on a grocery store shelf, by the toilet - it didn't matter - it was coming off! Looking back, I was definitely onto something.

I learned to cope and one way was by having an imaginary friend. Fonzie went with me everywhere but most importantly to my treatment appointments. We opted to try shots once a month for 3 months at the advice of a dermatologist. It was a spring-loaded shot that would pop the top of my head to administer a dose of cortisone. The sound of that shot hitting my skull is unforgettable. I can't think of a single sound that resembles it, and I can still hear it nearly 35 years later.

After three months of watching me suffer through these injections, my Mom made a bold decision to cease treatment. It wasn't working. After ending the cortisone shots, we tried applying cortisone cream to my scalp each night before bed.

I have a memory of taking what seemed like 30 vitamins at night as I watched television. One night, I accidentally swallowed the ginormous chewable vitamin and chewed the one I should have swallowed. It was a nasty, nearly-made-me-choke-to-death, life-changing memory that never left me.

While my Mom focused on covering it up or seeking treatment, my Dad couldn't bear the pain of not being able to fix it. Through the years, I have pieced together tender and angry words to realize that for some reason my Dad blamed himself. I think he blamed himself for it happening and hated himself for not being able to fix it. When this happened, I misinterpreted his hatred of himself as hatred of me.

I believe that the pain of possibly losing me was more than my Daddy could bear. He did not want to face that possibility, so he disconnected emotionally from me. There are so many photos of my Dad and my sister as a toddler. She was Daddy's little girl and my brother was Mama's boy. What was I? The bald kid with no future?

I thought my Dad hated me, but he didn't. He couldn't fix me. I was oblivious to the future I faced having Alopecia but he wasn't. I think about my own children. How when I see them make a mistake, I see the long-term consequence, but they see the immediate benefit.

My Dad saw one of two scenarios playing out: Worst case scenario was that I'd die, and best case scenario was that I would live a sad, sickly life, most likely alone.

My Daddy loved Gospel music. We would go as a family to all-night Gospel singings. There was a group that was his favorite, the Singing Americans. I had never seen my Daddy show any real emotion except when his mother died. He was a tough guy.

One night, at a Singing Americans concert, the group had two brothers, Michael and Biney English, who sang a song called, "Who Am I," written by Rusty Goodman. As they sang the words "Who am I that a King would bleed and die for," tears rolled down my Daddy's face.

I watched him watch them and longed to have that kind of pull on his heart. I wanted that kind of love from my Father.

It's so funny that I felt so unloved by my Dad in my teen years. I look back and want to smack myself in the back of the head. He showed me love in so many ways that I didn't understand.

For example, we tried allergy shots to make me feel better. I had serious allergy and sinus issues, maybe from not having hair in my ears, nose or eyelashes. We tried to use allergy shots to relieve the discomfort.

Twice a week, Daddy drove me to the doctor to get these shots. He would always treat me to a Mountain Dew and a Slim Jim. It was our thing, what we did. In fact, anytime I am feeling sick or down, nothing makes me feel better than a Mountain Dew and a Slim Jim.

Another thing he did was when I wanted to be a singer, he took me to voice lessons every week and paid for them. He would sit out in the truck while I went it for hour-long voice and stage lessons. I don't know if I ever thanked him, but those voice lessons taught me to stand up for myself. They taught me to be bold and that I was somebody.

My voice teacher, Scott Whitener, did something during the first lesson that really shocked me. He shoved me. I was standing there singing, and he shoved me. I fell back and lost my balance. He told me that the stage was mine; I shouldn't let anyone push me around.

Each week, he would shove me. Each week, I would lose my balance. Then one week, I barely stumbled. Not too long after that, I didn't even flinch when he would shove me. In fact, I would keep singing as if he wasn't even there. I learned to stand my ground. I carried this through my life. The world is my stage. My life is my performance. No one will push me around. I will not lose my grip on the world because someone is pushing me. That's a lesson for you right there, but there's another lesson.

We all have a love language, and I think my Dad's may be in acts. He did so many things, unselfishly for me. My love language back then was through words. He was telling me he loved me in his actions, and I was standing there waiting to hear him say it.

Change your world, resolve to be the better person and show love to the unlovable. I loved my Daddy in spite of his emotional detachment from me. We fought and had our issues, as you will read in other chapters, but when I was 21 years old, he told me he loved me for the first time. Since that day, I've been a Daddy's girl, and my sister has had to learn to share.

Tell the people in your life that you love them and tell them often. I resolved to never let a day go by that I didn't tell my children that I loved them. I tell them everyday still and have done so since they were born.
If we are angry with each other or having a bad day, we will not withhold those three words from each other. Never let anyone wonder how you feel about them, say "I love you" and say it often, without hesitation.

The world needs more love. A true world changer knows that.

NOTICED

My condition that started as Alopecia Areata (bald spots) turned into Alopecia Totalis (total hair loss on the head) when I was nine. Remember now, the hairstylist told my Mom to keep me from seeing the spots. I literally had no idea that I was going bald!

One day as I was standing in a line outside the library at school, the kid behind me asked me why I had a bald spot on my head. I was shocked. Surely this kid must be wrong. I reached to the back of my head and felt the spot.

I showed it to Mom when she got home from work and she finally told me that my hair was falling out. Everything, the shots, pills, treatments, creative hairstyling: it all made perfect sense to me at last.

I was nine years old, going bald and there were no other ways to part my hair in a way that covered it up. We had a family member die. While we were all gathered together after the funeral, my aunt told my Mom that she had bought me a wig. The next day, we went to her salon to try it on.

She called it a "blonde Annie wig." To me, it looked more like a "grey Granny wig." It was a short curly used wig that is as hideous to me now as it was then. I have no idea what made my aunt or my Mother think that this was an acceptable wig for a nine-year-old little girl. It has been more than 30 years since that day and I still can't look at pictures of me wearing that wig.

In that moment, there was no way that nine-year-old me was going to wear that thing. I mean, what would my boyfriend say? Then I realized an opportunity for negotiation for the first of many times, I walked away having won the debate.

I was (and still am) very competitive. I had been wanting to get my ears pierced, but my sister had to wait until she was 13 so I had to do the same. Looking at myself in the grey granny wig, I mentioned that I would be willing to wear it if my ears were pierced. Yes, I went there and that was the first time I played the Alopecia Card. In fact, this is a self-motivated version of "Alopecia Perks."

After we returned home from our trip to the funeral, I had to go back to school, but this time with my new hairdo. Just to recap, I was nine years old wearing a wig that was way older than me, but I have hope because I believe that my earrings will keep the attention off the wig. That morning, in the car, my Mom lied to me for the first and only time. She said to me, "No one will notice."

I remember I was wearing jeans that had flowers on the pocket. My scalloped collar blouse was tucked in and had a little red ribbon tied in a bow under the collar. My earrings really made the outfit.

Walking down the hall, headed to my fourth grade classroom, two teachers in a doorway whispered and giggled as I passed them. That was the moment I knew I was in trouble. If the teachers noticed and laughed, what were the students going to do? That was the first time that I looked down at my feet when I walked.

I walked in the classroom and someone noticed my wig before I even got to my desk. In fact, as I walked in the door, he yelled, "Laura's wearing a wig!"

This particular boy terrorized me. He most likely has no memory of the events of that year and many to follow, but he set a standard that others tried to top. He pulled my wig off once and would tell others that he had done it. I would walk down the hallway and hear the kids behind me daring each other to pull my wig off. This treatment continued on all the way to high school and drove me to a very dark place. However, that story is reserved for the next chapter.

The following Spring, one year into wearing wigs, we went to Florida to visit my mother's parents. My grandfather was a retired Baptist Minister and we all went to church with them for Easter morning. We arrive for Sunday School and I walk in looking at my feet. My grandmother (I called her EE - my toddler version of Granny) walked me up to the front of the classroom full of kids and introduced me.

She said, and I quote, "This is my Granddaughter Laura, she is bald and wears a wig but that's ok. Tell them what I told you Laura." Well, I looked up from my feet really quickly to look at her like she had lost her mind! She said, "you know - about Jesus." I posed my answer as more of a question to her than as an answer to the class, "If Jesus wanted me to have hair, I'd have hair?" "Yes," she said, "that's right. Now go have a seat."

I was mortified. What had she done? More than what, why? On the inside, I was totally freaking out. I trusted her. I loved her. But now I could never show my face in Florida again.

Truthfully though, she was so ahead of me. Every time I stand in front of a crowd and tell my story, I think of her. Even though she totally outed me, she meant so much to me. I wish I could thank her. I wish she could see me walking around bald and tell me, "I told you so."

If I had picked up the gift she put before me that day and wore that boldness without reservation, I could have prevented so much heartache for me and others. I could have changed the world. She opened the door to something incredible for me and I shut it out of fear.

It's okay to be afraid. Just don't let your circumstance suffocate your valor. When an opportunity presents itself for you to change the world, go forth with boldness. Lift your head and be confident that everything you need to stand up for what is right is in you already. Take it and be the change.

Actually, I want to go a step further.

Promise me that as of this very moment, you will never look at your feet again. Well, you can look at your feet to put on your shoes, but in life, you look forward, never down on yourself or anyone else. Be great like EE knows you are destined to be.

The story of EE is not the only situation in my life where someone tried to make me greater than I was. In junior high school, I met a wonderful bully. He was new, and on his first day he was assigned the seat in front of me. His name was Daniel. I knew I could sit behind him without incident because he was too new to know I wore a wig and, therefore, too new to make fun of me. New kids were safe until someone filled them in. I confidently took the seat behind him.

He turned around, and the first words out of his mouth were, "Hey there Wigwam!" Seriously? His first day and someone has already told him that I wore a wig. How cruel of a person to make fun of me right out of the gate!?! I crumpled in defeat. I didn't answer him; I just bowed my head down and tried to disappear and fight back the tears.

I had gotten really good at this by now.

I didn't realize that this was going to be a turning point in my life. With one statement, this person, who I labeled as "bully," was about to light a fire of confidence in me that would carry me to my adulthood. He quickly said to me (with confusion and hurt in his eyes)...

"If that's not something you are ok with joking about, why did you let me get away with it? Don't ever let anybody make you feel that way." Then he said, "Look at me! You should have totally fired back with a fat joke."

Funny Story! He gave me a word to call him and at the time (in our youth) we didn't know it was a sexually explicit word. I would yell this word out at him in the hallway. He thought it meant overweight. It didn't. We laughed about it a little while ago when I googled the word.

Daniel passed away in 2015. He spoke humor into being bald and having to wear a wig to school. He told me to hold my head high when people said stupid things. He was someone who everyone liked, and I was fortunate enough to call him my friend.

I did listen to Daniel. I took his advice to heart and learned to laugh about my situation.

I love to joke around and laugh. I think it might just be my hobby. So finding out that it was acceptable to take my situation lightly was very healing for me. Not everyone is comfortable with finding humor in a sad situation. You have to learn to roll with it.

I know that my humor is not a defense mechanism but rather a real personality trait that I possess. That isn't true for everyone. Using humor as a defense mechanism is a very real coping measure. The idea behind this is that if I can get you laughing with me, it might make you stop laughing at me.

I used to say that when I laughed the world laughed with me, but when I cried, the world kept laughing. I know that's a sad statement to make, but it felt very true to me. This was a statement so real before I came out bald. When I covered up with a wig, I felt like everyone was talking about it and laughing at me. I laughed publicly and cried privately. Basically, they didn't laugh at my pain, just at my expense. That was devastating to me.

Learn to identify this defense mechanism trait in others and give as much acceptance as you do laughter. They are merely making you laugh in an effort to make you love them. If a person makes a joke about a painful situation, don't keep the joke going. Instead, laugh along and then acknowledge the hurt that resulted.

CAN'T

Today, as I am sending my youngest child, my daughter, off to middle school, the words of everyone I've talked to lately are haunting me, "Middle school was the hardest!" To most people, that means changing classes was confusing, locker combination locks were difficult or homework is so much harder. For me, it meant the bullying went beyond what I imagined it could. Middle school kids were horrible!

The teen years were some of the hardest years for me. That's when hair starts becoming a defining feature of your beauty. Looking back at the hairstyles of the early 90's, now it feels I was spared, but it didn't feel that way at the time.

As my friends (and bullies) were combing their bangs up and spraying them high, I couldn't do so without exposing that my hair was a wig. Wigs were really thick then, and if I tried curling it or teasing it, my hair only got bigger.

Banana clips were my breaking point! They combed against the scalp too close into the hairdo and nothing I tried worked. That stupid little piece of plastic, a hairstyle that is quite ugly when you think about it, caused me so much heartache. You suck, banana clip!

That felt so good to say out loud. Go ahead, say it. You'll feel so much better.

The kids were so cruel to me. As I mentioned before, they would follow me through the hallways daring each other to touch or even pull off my wig. If they asked me if I was wearing a wig, I always denied it. That just made matters worse. Occasionally someone would tug enough to move it, and once it was completely pulled off and thrown on the ground.

We tried to find ways to make it stick. We used tapes and glues made for wigs that would keep it in place but not make it impossible to pull off. My brother worked for a plant that made industrial grade velcro. I'm not sure exactly what it was used for, but I'm sure it could connect the cars of a freight train together! This was strong Velcro, and the adhesive was even stronger. We had a moment of genius (or so we thought) when Benny brought some home to see if it would prevent my wig from being pulled off.

We cut small pieces of the Velcro off of the large roll and stuck one side on my head and then stuck the other side to the corresponding sections of the wig. This made the wig velcroed to my head at my temples and then at the base of my neck. What can I say, it worked. If you tugged the wig, it didn't budge. The first week I wore it, I was so confident knowing no one could pull off the wig. Until...

One day, I came home and pulled the wig off my head and the wig velcro stuck to the head Velcro a little too tight and it ripped the strip of Velcro from my head. When the strip ripped off, it took a chunk of skin with it. This meant I had a painful irritated spot on my head that was more irritated when wearing the wig. Until I healed, I would sit in school miserable! This also meant no more Velcro.

I went back to living in fear. daily of having my wig pulled off. In fact, I still have the scar on the right side of my head where the velcro ripped off. It's quite a bummer of a story anytime I tell how I got the scar.

I was fortunate though because I didn't have to face any of this alone. I had, who I will refer to as the best friend love of my life, Denise to lean on and fight beside.

A friend had invited a new girl at school to my sleepover hoping she would make a friend or two before the school year started. It was my 12th birthday and as a gift, Denise gave me a ticket to go with her to Carowinds (a Paramount Theme park) the next day. We had just met, but we immediately hit it off and spent the entire day laughing.

I don't remember ever telling Denise I wore a wig or why. She just knew and accepted me into her life without hesitation. I would do anything for her and she for me. Her family from her parents to her aunts, uncles and cousins became my family. I would joke that she was the sister I never had. My sister didn't like that joke, but it made me laugh.

I love this woman. I don't know that I have a single childhood memory that doesn't involve Denise or her family. Her parents welcomed me into their home, on their family vacations and even reprimanded me when I needed it as if I was flesh and blood. My best friend life with Denise was a reprieve from the reality that I was different and didn't belong. When I met Denise, I found a place to belong.

That's my formal introduction of Denise to you. You will read snippets about her throughout the book, but know when you read about her, she is a wonderful friend. I know that if God had not placed her in my life, I would not be upright today.

Back to going to school dealing with the drama that is wearing a wig in junior high school.

This was a small town in the South, and the white kids and the black kids didn't necessarily play together. Unlike today, I didn't grow up with a lot of black friends but had never understood the idea of this friendship segregation. In junior high school, as the white kids were teasing me, I was taken by surprise at how supportive and kind the black kids were to me.

I remember two occasions. Once in the gym during a pep rally, these white girls were picking on me. A black girl, that I didn't know, walked up to me and told me those white girls are saying I was wearing a wig. Before I could stop her, she reached towards my wig, and I thought she was going to pull it off.

She tugged it lightly and then looked up at the white girls and yelled, "She ain't wearing no wig. Leave her alone. You're so stupid!"

A similar incident happened with a black guy. I was friends with his sister, but he had a bit of a reputation. He came and told me that the kid I mentioned earlier that pulled my wig off was telling everyone about it.

This kid was creating a challenge of sorts to top him. He had pulled my wig off and now others wanted to. I am sure he could see the fear in my eyes. He called the other kid a liar and along with his friends, they heckled him until he retreated.

I can't explain why these individuals came to my rescue. They didn't know me. We didn't walk in the same crowds. They created a loyalty from me though. I've always been able to relate to the entire black race. I see them as a sort of hero in my childhood. My black knights in shining armor.

That's been true with many minorities in my life, including the LGBTQ community. They get what it's like to be different and be judged for it; they get me. They have my back and I will always have theirs.

In an effort to belong or be popular, I decided to tryout for cheerleading. I had a bubbly personality and was tall and thin and quite loud. It seemed like a perfect fit for me. Tryouts consisted of staying after school for a few days in mock rehearsals while the cheer coach and some current cheerleaders taught us a series of cheers and dances. I don't know why I ever thought this was a good idea.

On tryout day, I was in it to win it. I was probably horrible at it but remember, I've always had this idea in my head that I could do anything. On this day, I knew I'd make that team. My time came to "perform," and I immediately regretted my decision. What if my wig flew off? Everyone would know (because in my mind, no one could tell)! My routine went off without any issues, and I bopped my way back in the line.

They asked all of us girls to step into the hallway while they deliberated. I ran to the restroom really quickly and while I was in the stall, I heard two girls (current cheerleaders) talking at the sinks. They were talking about different girls and my name came up. One girl said she hoped I didn't make it because it would be embarrassing if my wig came off during a game. The other girl agreed and said that would be humiliating.

It would be humiliating. For them? Humiliating for the cheerleaders if MY wig came off during a game? What about me? What about how it would make me feel if my wig came off during a game? What about how I felt panic just trying out fearing my wig would fall off but was strong and brave and faced my fear anyway?

I don't know if I was good or not, probably not. I didn't make the team. I don't know if ability or fear of embarrassment was why I didn't make the team.

Regardless of the reason, I took away that I didn't make the team because I would be an embarrassment to them if I did. That was one of many times that I saw Alopecia as a handicap when it isn't.

Another time was in high school when I thought

for a fleeting moment about trying out for the swim team. I'm not confident in my cheering skills, but I am still a good swimmer. This I knew I could do! The meeting to join was in a classroom immediately following the last class of the day. I headed straight to the classroom and it felt right.

The coach seemed great and there was no tryout process. Most of the kids on the team were kids that I didn't normally hang out with, and I thought this could be a great way to meet them. Most were the wealthier, preppy class of students. As the coach was detailing what happened on swim meet days, I was imagining myself prepping for the meet.

I'd arrive at the school and we'd ride together on the bus to the pool for the competition. We'd change into our swimsuits there in the locker room and put all of our belongings in a duffle and the coach would lock them up in a room.

I figured out a few things:

1. I may not always have privacy when changing from wig to swim cap.
2. You would be able to tell there was no hair under the swim cap.
3. If we had the same bags, someone could open mine by mistake and see my wig.
4. As I looked around the room at the boys, some of whom had made fun of

me, I realized they would have access to my wig in the duffle bag in the room.

5. If my cap came off during a meet and everyone saw my bald head, my team would be humiliated by me.

I left that day and never went back. I didn't even try. The fear of my secret being exposed and me being ridiculed stopped me from pursuing something in which I could have possibly excelled. This wasn't the only thing. There were other activities I was interested in, basketball and track for example, that I made no effort to pursue. Why would I?

Even if I made it, my wig might come off and they would be humiliated.

I became extremely depressed to the point of being suicidal. I would lay in bed at night, crying myself to sleep and pray that I wouldn't wake up in the morning. One night, I couldn't take another walk in the hallway at school or another night of crying myself to sleep, and I knew I was done.

I had this powder/pill form of an asthma inhaler. It was noted (and reported through the news) that taking more than eight or so a month could be life threatening. One night, determined to not face another day, I took about 24.

As I was inhaling the powder of these pills, a friend of mine called me. I don't know why I answered the phone. Looking back, that is so baffling to me.

Why in the world would I answer the phone as I am trying to end my life? I did answer it though, and it was a friend of mine who told me to stop what I was doing. She said she had been awakened from her sleep and felt led to say that to me.

This was not a church going, Christian believer that you would expect this from. In fact, I'm not even sure she believed in God at all. Yet, God used her that day to save my life.

I'm so thankful that I had people who loved me enough to reach me. She's a Facebook friend and every time I see a post from her, I'm reminded of what she did for me.

A disadvantage to having an autoimmune disorder is the unpredictable nature of my body's response to being exposed to any given virus. One night, after being in the studio working on my second Gospel album, I notice I had a bump on my arm that itched really badly. I showed it to my Mom and we both joked that it looked like a solitary chicken pock. Those start on your stomach though so we assumed I was safe.

Until I woke up the next morning covered from head to toe.

Have you had the Chicken Pox? Remember how horrible they were? Imagine having them at 16 years old. I stayed home from school the first day, and we laughed about how I found myself 16 years old with the Chicken Pox. By day three or so, we stopped laughing and went to the Doctor for help.

I had Chicken Pox on every inch of my body. Every inch, as in eyelids, inside my nose, inside my ears, anywhere that had skin. The Doctor recommended we try an oatmeal bath and let it run its course.

Its course, with my autoimmune disordered body, was a little over two weeks. I couldn't return to school until they had started healing and the fever was gone.

By the time I reached that point, two weeks later, I had missed quite a bit of school. I worked really hard at making up my work. I had an afterschool job to pay for my car and my car insurance. Missing work was not an option. My teachers were the best and they worked with me every morning before school to get my work caught up.

I was so proud to find myself, even after all of that missed school, making straight A's in my classes. The week of report cards for the first semester, I was called to the Principal's office. That was strange for me. I had NEVER been called to see the Principal. I knew I hadn't done anything wrong. I remember wondering if I had won a prize or something. Nothing prepared me for what happened next.

I sat down in the Principal's office and he very coldly informed me that I had missed more than the allowable amount of days. As a result, I would receive an "F" in every class that semester. To make matters worse, this would ultimately mean that I would fail the 11th Grade and have to repeat it next year.

Here I was, first semester of the school year, and I had no chance of passing.

I tried to explain to him that I had come to school early every morning, truly believing this was a mistake that this explanation would fix it. He was a jerk, really.

Looking back on that day, "No Child Left Behind" must have not been a thing yet. Without any emotion or desire to see me succeed, he claimed that coming in before school did not count. I had to make up my time after school. Furthermore, I had to make up 2 weeks' worth of time, which couldn't be done in 4 days.

I told some of my friends about my plight and shared with them that I was considering dropping out of school. Okay, don't freak out. I know what you are thinking and I agree. Calm down and read on. I have a happy ending, and I am not writing a book to condone dropping out of school. Now back to my story.

I had shared my intentions with some friends, and one of them decided to seek help from a teacher in hope of an intervention. As I was standing at the salad bar to get my lunch, a teacher from my 10th grade year walked up behind me and whispered the following in my ear:

"I know what you are planning to do. I am going to tell you something and if you say I told you this, I will deny it. If anyone can quit school and be successful, it's you. Promise me you will keep writing."

Then she disappeared in the sea of high school kids eating lunch.

I went home and talked it over with my parents, and we decided that the best option was for me to quit high school. It was a Tuesday, and I slept late for two reasons:

1. I didn't want to face the students going into school as I am there to quit.
2. If I was quitting, there was no reason NOT to sleep late.

I started with the front desk. I told the receptionist my name and that I was there to "quit school." She asked me to have a seat and she called the Counselor. The School Counselor was a fantastically nice lady from what I understood. Everyone loved her. I had no experience with her. Here I was, a child that was suicidal, had even tried to kill myself and was bullied daily, and this was my first time in her office.

As I was talking with her, I kept my composure and used my inner Attorney to plead my case. She tried tough love and that just made me flip my care switch. Getting nowhere with me, she called my mother - my mother, who had quit high school to marry my father who also quit high school. She asked my mother if she knew what I was doing and Mom told her she did. The words she said next never left me. They served as a motivator and a depressor at the same time.

She told my mother, "You know your daughter will be another statistic and will never amount to anything." She went on to paint a picture of me spending my days in the unemployment line. When you compare the words of this faculty member to the words of the teacher who stopped me in the lunchroom, the comparison is incredible. I'd like to think that the words of the latter were my moving force but they were not even thought of during this moment.

She then told me that in order to quit school, it was required that I go to each teacher and have them sign a paper saying I had turned in my book to him or her.

I was being bullied and tormented, was suicidal and saw quitting school as a way out and was now being forced to walk into several different classrooms and explain my situation to each of my teachers for all of the students to hear.

A few of the teachers signed my paper without saying anything. Two of them questioned why I was being made to do this as a child had never been made to do it before me. One hugged me and wished me the very best.

That was the worst case of bullying that I had ever endured. It was harsh and when I got back into my car, I let the tears pour that I had been holding back.

I felt so humiliated and defeated. At the same time, I cried out of relief that it was finally over. The days of walking through the hallways in fear were no more. It was like tons of weight had been lifted.

I quit school because of a hiccup in their rules. I did so without hesitation or regret because I was finally free of the bullies.

So many other things happened during this ordeal. I could probably write a book about just this one situation. The school board was brought in to investigate and, from what I understand, the rules have been changed. Years later, the Principal was terminated for reasons I do not know.

So considering all of the above, it came time to leave school and heal, physically and mentally. It was not an easy decision, and it was very risky, but it saved my life.

I mentioned already that I didn't date much. I didn't think I was ugly though. I wasn't delusional by any means, but I thought I might even be pretty.

So one day, I got it in my head that I was going to model. I needed something to fall back on because of the whole "high school dropout" path.

I set up a meeting with the Stone Modelling Agency. I arrived early, signed in and sat down in the waiting room. As I was waiting in a room with some other models, Ms. Libby Stone herself walked through, looked at me and said, "You're beautiful. Are you a model?" She signed me that day and agreed to train me since I had no modelling experience.

Now I know you've all heard of the "modelling schools," but Libby's was much different. The school fee came out of pay from actual modelling jobs. She taught this as a finishing school, not just modelling. I learned so much from Ms. Stone.

In fact, when I present to a crowd or go on a job interview, I still use the skills she taught me. I had back surgery in 2005. Following surgery, the physical therapist told me that I had the best posture she had ever seen. I smiled as I remembered Libby breaking me of my bad posture.

Speaking of jobs and presentations, I'm very happy to report that I did get my GED and later in life got a college degree. I've worked at law firms and production companies. While a radio promoter, the industry voted and named me the 1999 SGMA Radio Promoter of the Year. I'm currently Marketing Director for an International Organization, and I own my own agency. I travel telling my story under the moniker, The Bald Marketer.

Now, I think it's time for a lesson. This Chapter has three lessons - buckle up!

Don't let your mistakes or missteps define who you can be.

I'm a high school dropout. I shouldn't have had the success I have or be in the career I am in. Statistically, I should be working a minimum wage job or not at all. Here's the problem with following statistics: When these numbers are compiled, they do not consider the human element of the results.

How many high school dropouts are extremely intelligent and could have done more without a diploma than most people can do with a degree?

How many of them gave up because they bought into the lies that they were worthless without that piece of paper? How would their stories have been altered if they had never known that they were destined to fail?

If there is a mistake, decision or path that has created a roadblock in your path to greatness, knock it down, jump over it or dance across it. Decide right now that you are capable of doing anything you put your mind to. Let nothing stop you! Trust me, I know! Take it from this New York Times' Best Selling author who has a GED. (I told you I was a dreamer.)

If you find yourself in charge of shaping the future of another, do so with responsibility and regard for their heart.

This is big. If you are in a position that you influence the life of another human being - parents, teachers, managers, c-level executives, pastors, doctors and basically everybody else - I'm talking to you! One thoughtless word spoken in a moment of frustration (or as in my case in an effort to use fear tactics to get your way) can have a damaging effect on the future of the person receiving your unsubstantiated opinion.

I've always said I consider the heart of the advice when I receive it. I ask myself, "what heart is this person saying this in?" Is it from a place of genuine concern for my well-being or is it from a place of jealousy or desire to cause hurt? Make sure you speak from the right heart when you try to predict the abilities or potential of another person.

Your life matters and this bad patch will pass.

I made a decision when I didn't die from the suicidal attempt (I forgot to tell you I lived but I assume that is well... assumed), I decided that I would NEVER let myself get to a point that taking my life was an option. I remove negative people and negative situations from my life if they take me to that place.

Nothing will ever be that big in my life. It's a conscious decision I made and one that I make daily. You need to do this in your own life. If you take your life, you are not only hurting everyone that loves you (even if they don't tell you) but you are also killing any potential that this world needs from you. Turn that hurt and fear into something positive. Use it to reach someone and help someone else through their situation.

It breaks me to hear of kids taking their lives because they are different or bullied. When someone doesn't accept you for who you are for any reason, remember that their acceptance means nothing. It is your self acceptance that will make you strong and make you great. If you find yourself desperate or feeling unaccepted for any reason, email me. You matter to me.

MOVES

I have a confession to make. I'm a really good flirt. Like I can come up with an impressive pick-up line on the spot! As a teenager, meeting boys outside of my network of people, basically boys who didn't know I wore a wig, was too easy for me. It's surprising I stayed as innocent as long I did. Well, I'll explain that later.

I was married for 20 years and have recently found myself single again, so maybe my pick-up skills can be put to good use. I should probably write a fictional series on dating. It would sell like hot cakes. That or I could start a dating advice service like that movie Hitch starring Will Smith. If you ever meet me, ask me about it and I'll share one of my classic lines with you.

Back to the point...

I guess people saw me as pretty at the time. I look back at pictures post braces and I see a pretty girl that was so sad because she couldn't seem to get a boyfriend. I would flirt, first date, and meet lots of times but nothing more. I had a rule of not dating boys that knew about my hair. You know what, I take that back. I think it was that boys that knew about my hair had a rule about not dating me.

Once during a church youth party, I was sitting on the floor and heard a boy behind me say, "she'd be pretty if she didn't wear that wig." I remember having two thoughts:

1. He said I would be pretty.
2. No matter how pretty my wig is, I'm ugly because of it.

One time I had a crush on a boy in Junior High. He was one year younger than me but really tall. I thought he was SOOO cute. I would smile and whisper when he was looking. He is the first boy that I went to school with that I wanted to ask if he liked me. I don't know why I trusted him and trusted my classmates to think it would end well.

In the end, he was a good guy. He didn't like me because I wore a wig. I suspect it was the fear of what his friends would say more than a like or dislike of me personally.

Again, I had to hear a boy say that I was pretty but "wore a wig." The most hurtful part of the situation was that someone I thought was my friend had told him about my hair in an effort to make him not like me. She liked him.

Two more lessons learned as a result of this experience.

1. I never again told a boy from school that I liked him.
2. I was very careful who I called friend.

Only talking to boys that didn't know about my hair created an irrational fear of intimacy. I was afraid to kiss a boy much less do anything else. I was so scared that the boy would try to run his fingers through my hair and either pull off my wig or get his fingers caught in it. Realistically, this is a very rational fear and possible scenario. Talk about a mood killer! I avoided the first kiss as long as I could. Then, at 17 years old, I had to literally take one for the team.

Remember Denise, my best friend since I was 12 years old, like my sister to me? To this day, we are still close. I laugh when I look back on our years as teenagers. Just about every instance of flirting or meeting a boy involved Denise in some way. Either her sending me to the frontline to make the introduction or using my abilities in our favor.

One summer, Denise and I had met boys during a beach trip, best friends themselves. Denise's boy was super cute and looked like Ashton Kutcher. His friend looked like Goose from Top Gun. Denise was shy, and I was not so she got a brilliant idea, "If you kiss his friend, maybe he will kiss me." I'm always up for a dare but in this case I kissed Goose so Denise could kiss Ashton.

My first kiss was a mercy kiss and it was horrific. This poor boy really needed some help. He practically washed my face! I was so underwhelmed by the experience. Denise was so happy because her cute guy was a good kisser. Later in the book when you read about the sacrifice that Denise makes me for me, remember this story. She owed me big time!

I don't consider that my first romantic kiss though. It did serve as a learning experience of what worked. I figured out that if I put my hands on the boy's neck & face, the boy automatically put his hands on my waist. That meant no fingers tangled up in my wig, which was a big win for me.

Not too much longer after the goose face kiss, Denise and I were in a store shopping when we saw the cutest boy that looked like Johnny Depp, Benny and Joon era. We scoped him out before heading out to the food court for some lunch.

We were sitting down for only a few minutes when he sat at a table near us. Denise noticed that he was pretending to read while actually watching me. We giggled, hung around him as much as we could without being creepy, and reluctantly left without meeting him.

We were in the car leaving when I exclaimed, "Take me back!"

I walked in the store and spotted him after only a few minutes. I walked up to him and said, "So what was your plan? Were you just going to stare at me or actually talk to me?" He was so glad I spoke to him and he got my number and called me soon thereafter.

He lived more than an hour away from me but would come pick me up for dates. This is who I credit as my first kiss. Oh wow, when we were married, I used to tell my husband that he owed this boy so much appreciation. Everything I know about kissing, I learned from him. He is Italian and that boy could kiss.

We ultimately stopped seeing each other because I pulled away as a result of my fear of intimacy. I couldn't tell him I wore a wig, and if he tried to get close physically, I would resist.

I would like to add that when MySpace was big, I added him and he sent me the sweetest message. He told me about how some of his fondest days was when he drove to Stanley, NC to see me. Then he added that he wished I would have told him that I wore a wig. To him, it would have never mattered.

Me too, friend, I wish I had told you.

I didn't tell him, and we faded into nothing. About that time, a friend of mine had invited me to a music event with about 25,000 fans in attendance. It was a gospel group that she loved! She also loved a certain gospel singer and when she discovered he was sitting in a sky box watching the show, we walked up to say, "hello." He was very nice to her and another man came out and briefly spoke to us.

As we walked away, I asked about him. She told me his name and that he was married. Alright then... never mind. Little did I know that night, that he was going through a divorce and that the man I noticed would one day be my husband.

My friend introduced me to him (the man I saw but didn't pursue) a few months later because he was a music consultant and she thought he could help me with my own singing career. We went to dinner one night to discuss the possibility of working together.

I got brave and decided not to let me wearing a wig stop me this time. I told him that I was bald and that I wore a wig. He said, "I already knew." Someone else in the industry, gossiping of course, had told him that I wore a wig. He assured me that it didn't matter, most performers do.

What he didn't tell me is that he didn't eat the rolls that night or keep his leftovers from dinner because he wasn't sure if Alopecia was contagious or not! Seeing as we were married for nearly 20 years and had three children, he obviously got over that!

On our very first date, a huge gush of wind hit us as we were walking through the parking lot. My wig went flying off my head and rolled on the ground like a tumbleweed. Just like ten years before when that kid in school pulled off my wig, I stood there holding my bald head trying to cover it up with my hands while my wig blew away. He ran after my wig and caught it. He brought it to me and I quickly placed it back on my head.

On February 9, 1997, I was shocked to find myself pregnant. I had been told I would never have children because I would most likely go through menopause before I was 18. (More of that medical nonsense associated with Alopecia.) We spent the day discussing what we would do and finally decided to make it official.

We got married on Valentine's Day 1997. Our marriage ended officially in October of 2016, but that is not a story I will be sharing in this book.

People have always asked me if I found myself single again, would I still not wear the wig? Here I am single again and I most definitely continue to live my life free as a bald woman. If a person of interest does not accept that decision, I would lose interest quickly.

I've been told, it was never my hair that made me attractive. I've been told its my eyes, lips and skin. Not "she puts the lotion in the basket way" but my soft and clear skin. Alopecia perk maybe?

So what's the lesson in this chapter? You didn't figure it out? The lesson is that although I may not have been good at sports or popular, I could flirt! No, that's not the lesson.

The lesson is this. I allowed the fact that I wore a wig to keep me from letting others in emotionally and intimately. In some ways, that defense mechanism was a good thing but in other ways it kept me from accepting love from those who wanted to love me. The entire time I was caught up in what they would think about my hair that I didn't even realize that I had other qualities that drew them in.

If you're looking for love or a new career or even thinking of writing a book, don't let what you think is your downfall be your downfall. Look deep in yourself and find that thing that makes you lovable. That's what you need to focus on. Take that thing that makes you different and let it make you great.

I don't even know you and I love you. How about giving the rest of the world a chance to do the same? There just might be someone, somewhere waiting on someone just like you. Be you.

ADJUSTED

In my early 20's, I felt a little lost. I was no longer travelling as a Gospel singer. I wasn't writing at all. I worked as a Radio Promoter and basically spent my days promoting the talents of other creative people. I felt a little lost. Most importantly, I couldn't shake the feeling that there was more to my life than this.

It was during this time that I had some pretty devastating (to me) things happen that left me more self conscious than ever. It seemed like everywhere I went, someone was coming up to me and asking me if I was wearing a wig. It was so humiliating to me.

While visiting a zoo with my family, we were laughing and walking around enjoying our day, when these two older ladies (old enough to know better) were obviously talking about me. They would whisper and giggle while looking my way.

This was before I was the opinionated, loud spoken, jokester that I am now. I just took it and kept walking. At the same time, I walked in a way that I hoped would keep me hidden from their pointing.

Here they come! They started walking towards me and right in front of my children, they asked me if I was wearing a wig. I gave them my rehearsed answer of, "no it's not" and as I am answering, one of them reached up and rubs a section of my hair between her fingers. She turned to the woman beside her and announced, "yes – it's a wig!" They both stood there talking about me to each other as if I wasn't there.

Now, I'm going to say this. I WISH somebody would do that to me now. I would put on a comedy like none they have ever seen. That and I would totally film it and put it on YouTube. That day, however, I cried.

In another instance I was attempting to have lunch with my husband in a popular fast food establishment whose mascot has red pigtails. I say attempting because what was a quick break for lunch turned into an ordeal that ruined my day, maybe my week.

I stepped up to the register to place my order, smile on my face, but before I could speak, the following interaction took place:

Her: Is that a wig?

Me: What? Why would you ask me that?

Her: See that man right there (pointing at a guy laughing at the fry grill)? He says he went to school with you and you wear a wig.

Me: Would you ask an amputee if he was wearing a fake leg?

Her: No. Is that a wig? That's a wig (laughing)!

I asked to see the manager and of course she lied to me that she was the manager. The place was packed and I was so humiliated. I sat down at the table and cried. I couldn't even tell my husband why I was so upset. He went up and got the food so that I didn't have to.

I really have no memory of what happened from the time I walked away from the conversation to the time we got back to the office. I think that my husband complained. I think we ate our food quickly and left. I honestly don't know. It was a fog. I zombied my way out of there and have never gone back to this day.

When I got back to the office, I wrote a letter to the corporate office and heard back from the area manager and the girl who insulted me. The manager made her write me a letter apologizing for her actions.

I still have the letter somewhere, and it had a great impact on me but not for the reason you would think.

The letter broke my heart. It wasn't well written. This wasn't someone who knew how to express herself in words, and it was full of misspellings. I was so ticked off at her but then I felt so bad for her at the very same time. It was a horrible way to feel. I really wanted to hate her. I wanted to insult her and make her feel as bad as she had made me feel. I wanted to go back into the restaurant and laugh at her for her sentence structure and inability to spell.

I couldn't do it though. After reading that letter, I just saw a hurting, struggling person who maybe didn't know better. Maybe this was one of many bad decisions that would keep her from ever living to her full potential. She broke me, twice.

Not every interaction about being bald or wearing a wig was a bad one. Once, after I had placed my order in a fast food line, I noticed the girl taking my order kept giving me dirty looks. Then she started throwing stuff down and was really mad at me.

Finally, after her frustration was evident to everyone, I asked her what I had done to upset her. She said, "You're standing there giving me dirty looks and I ain't done nothing to you!"

Honestly baffled by this, I caught my reflection in the glass of a photo and realized that I had drawn on what my kids would later refer to as "angry eyebrows."

I tried to explain this to her but she was so upset by this point there was no making it right. If you are reading this book, I am so sorry. I promise it was not intentional and I hope I didn't ruin your day.

So back to this empty feeling I was carrying around. I had two sons, Cross and Chaz. They fulfilled me from a love point of view but professionally, I was not moving forward. I had filled in that blank to be famous remember. I felt forgotten.

One night as I was sitting in the bed watching television, my 4-year-old son Cross came in and sat down beside me. He slipped his little neck under my arm and looked up at me with his bright blue eyes glaring at me. I could feel his stare.

He reached up to my bald head, rubbed his hand across it and gently said, "Mama – your hair is so pretty." I reminded him that I'm bald and he replied, "I know and it's so pretty."

That tender little conversation with a sensitive toddler wise beyond his years is to date the most defining moment in my life. We didn't say anything further beyond those words because we didn't have to.

For the first time in my life, I saw myself through his eyes. More importantly, I saw a door open up for me to do something great, and I walked through it. I made the decision that day to stop saying that I wasn't wearing a wig and to start telling my story.

For Cross' tenderness, Chaz brought humor into my situation. We took the boys to a toy store one Saturday close to Mother's Day. The store was hosting a craft event where children could make their Mother a gift for Mother's Day. My boys sat down and I walked away a few steps to allow them to make my gift "without me seeing it." I heard a commotion and turned around to find Chaz arguing with the lady helping him with his craft.

Remember, I wore wigs and no one knew I was bald. She was telling him to put brown yarn on his paper doll so it would look like his Mother. He yelled for her to leave him alone because he didn't want that brown yarn - his doll already looked like his Mama! They argued back and forth and I stepped in and asked her to let him make it his way. I laughed all the way home.

Years later, we had a daughter (finally) and she could carry in the tradition. Once in a church service, they called all the children up front for a lesson. They asked if any of the children had a prayer request and Lyvie said, "pray for my Mama cause y'all know she's bald." Thank God I was "out" as a bald woman by then or I would have had to hide and never go back to that church.

Oh the joys of Motherhood. Being a bald Mother to hairy kids is an adventure. When I was a little girl I told my Mother that God had promised me that when I grew up I would have a daughter. Growing up, I looked forward to having that daughter to fix her hair and watch her grow up to be beautiful. I was going to live vicariously through her.

I married a man who had two sons from a previous marriage. When we had our first ultrasound for our first child, I just knew it was going to be a girl.

They had told me I would never have children so I assumed this was a one shot miracle so it had to be that girl. As they told me it was a boy, I felt a tear roll down my face. It felt like God had broken his promise.

Then, baby #2 came to be and as I waited for the ultrasound, I told them not to tell me what I was having. I was convinced I could "faith" my way into a girl this time. I was looking at the screen and I saw it without them telling me. I busted out laughing at the sight of another boy. I thought to myself, "real funny God."

Years later, I found myself again laying on a table with goop on my stomach waiting on an ultrasound. The tech told us everything looked good and showed us the fingers and toes. Without skipping a beat or with any warning, she nonchalantly said, "so you're having a baby girl." We all gasped!

I yelled, "What did you say?" and then I made her prove it. A girl. She came into our life with a little girl cry that warned us from day one that she was delicate and tender. I named her Olyvia Cille. Cille is short for Voncile, my grandmother that shaped me.

With all three kids, I panicked many times thinking that a blonde patch of baby hair was a bald spot. I freaked out if one pulled the other's hair. I cried when a hair stylist cut their hair wrong and became furious when she validated it with, "Oh Mom, it's only hair. It'll grow back." I would lay awake at night afraid that tomorrow would be the day that Lyv's hair might fall out.

I've been asked how I would react if one of my children had Alopecia. I have two thoughts on this question. First of all, as I mentioned before, I wouldn't wish this condition on anyone. It would break my heart for one of my children to have to face it. I know the emotional weight of the stares, laughter and thoughtless comments of other people and I don't want that for my children.

However, I also know that life goes on. If I've done nothing else, I have raised my children to see people and not difference. I hope that my own journey would inspire them to see their own greatness beyond any circumstance. If that circumstance is Alopecia, we will get through it. After I've cried it out of course.

That's my message to you here. See people. Don't see weight, color, handicap, things – see people.

See that inside that person wearing the worn shoes and mismatch shirt is a human being that needs to be told that they matter. That guy that just asked you out, the one you would NEVER go out with, used up every ounce of his courage to talk to you. Treat him with kindness so that he has the courage to do that again. You may not be the one for him, but someone is. Don't ruin it for her.

OUT

After Cross opened my eyes that it was indeed ok to be different, I was on a mission to have my story heard. The Pastor's wife at the church I was attending created an event just for me to tell my story. It was a women's tea and I stood in front of a group of women and for the first time, publicly admitted that I was wearing a wig.

I told them that I had finally gotten to a place where I could accept it and like me, I wanted them to use their difference to make a difference in someone else's life. I decreed this challenge hoping to inspire these ladies. I told my story seeing my moment of glory at last.

I imagined as I told them about being bullied as a child, they should feel bad for me. They did.

I had high expectations that as I told them how depressed and suicidal I was they would shed tears of mourning. They did.

My grand finale was going to be after I was done telling my stories. I knew they would line up to talk to me to tell me how inspirational I was. How they admired me so much. They did. But...

The complement line didn't go as I had envisioned. One lady told me about how she had lost 5 babies, all stillborn at birth. Then she thanked me for reminding her that she wasn't alone in her hurt. Another woman, in an electric wheelchair, paralyzed from the neck down was next. With tears running down her face, she thanked me for telling her story.

My visions of grandeur and being the hero at this event faded into nothing. I learned this day that the world was bigger than me. These ladies had so much greater hurt than I did but they took the time to listen to my story and even relate to me. My hurt was nothing compared to theirs. Sound familiar?

I knew this was bigger than I even knew. This wasn't about me telling the world I'm bald; it was about me changing the world. Changing it to see that we are in this thing together and we are nothing without each other.

Go big or go home, right? Go big I did. I started by taking two huge steps in the direction of coming out bald.

First I contacted a photographer that I had met at an event. He had told me that he thought I looked like a Bond girl. Well, if he saw that in me, he got my business. I called him and reminded him of his offer to shoot me. I gave the request a twist by asking that he shoot me bald.

After explaining why/how I would be bald, he was all in and excited. On the day of the photo shoot, he taught me about fixing my eyebrows correctly, using my eyes to tell a story and that big earrings and bold lips are hot! We took hundreds of shots with my wig on and bald.

The day the photos arrived in the mail, they were so liberating. I kept getting the same response, the pictures of me in the wig were beautiful, but the ones of me bald were breathtaking. Literally, when I would show them to someone, I could hear them gasp when they got to the bald picture. I was shocked to discover that there was something pure, maybe even sexy, about being a bald woman.

Step two – take this story primetime. The best way to do that was on television. I loved TLC (the channel but the group too for that matter). They had a show called A Makeover Story that I would binge watch on Saturdays. I contacted them with a pitch.

Someone had seen me at an industry event, a gospel group of wonderful people, and they had noticed my wig looked bad. They donated the money to have a custom wig made for me.

I contacted TLC, told them about an awards show I was attending and explained how I did not know what to do with my hair. It worked! Boy did it work!

My story was chosen to be featured on what would become their first human interest episode. When I spoke to the production assistant on the phone to do the preliminary interview, she asked if I would be willing to go bald on the show. I immediately told her that I didn't feel comfortable doing that. She assured me that it wouldn't be asked of me, but that I should say yes so that the show would get approved.

Let me say, I have no issues with this experience. I don't want that part of the story to paint a bad picture of the experience. You'll see in a moment that it was the best thing that could have happened. We drove to Nashville, Tennessee and the show put us up in a Suite at the Opry Hotel.

It was so fantastic!

They met us in our suite for the first day of filming and as soon as the cameras were set up, the producer told me to go ahead and get ready to film the scene where I take off my wig. Panic hit me immediately but the studio and network had spent thousands of dollars on this episode; I couldn't back out now. Without giving it a second thought, I took that wig off on camera like a boss. I felt like I was in that classroom with EE all over again. She would have been proud.

We filmed all of the back story on the first day and visited a formal clothing store to buy my clothes and jewelry for the Dove Awards. I felt like a princess for the first time in my life. I never went to senior prom and I didn't have a wedding so this was significant to me.

The next morning started bright and early. We met at a salon and literally spent all day on hair, nails and makeup. This was the first time in my life that I had the salon hair experience. They strapped the wig on with a chin strap and washed it on my head. I finally understood why people love that so much. It felt wonderful.

They colored my hair a beautiful shade that had some red and caramel highlights in it. Then they cut it in a trendy style. That was the first time I had ever had hair that was anything close to being trendy. They even showed me how to fix the hair myself.

When we arrived in a limo with cameras following us around, the celebrities were treating us like celebrities. It was quite the magical experience. We knew it would be wonderful. I knew I would get a new outfit and the diva experience. I was prepared to see my story on TV and hoped it would get me some speaking engagements. What I didn't take into account was the public response and recognition.

Everywhere we went, someone would come up to us saying they had seen us on TLC. From flight attendants chatting me up in an elevator in Orlando, Florida to a woman buying groceries in Walmart. I joke that with my reality TV fame, I am the Kim Kardashian of the Alopecia community.

The wig that was donated and styled for the show was such a great wig. I took such special care of it. Then a moment that I can only compare to Michael Jackson catching his hair on fire, happened. My husband walked through the house gathering up dirty towels to throw in the washing machine and accidentally grabbed a towel that my wig was wrapped in after I had just washed it. It was the weekend before Denise's wedding (which I was in) and I had a washing system that included soaking up excess water with a towel before hanging the wig to dry.

He threw the towel containing my beautiful custom wig into a washing machine full of hot water and bleach. By the time we realized what had happened it was too late. The wig was melted together and looked exactly like a Furby. To say I freaked out would be an understatement. I'm pretty sure I hyperventilated.

We found a wig shop in the mall near my in-law's house in Hickory, NC and called ahead to make sure they were open. I had a wrap on that covered my head but there was no way I was going to walk through the mall wearing that wrap. You could tell I was bald.

Do you understand what I am saying? I literally took my wig off on National Television to 12 million viewers but couldn't walk through a mall without a wig without totally freaking out.

My husband and his mother went into the mall and asked the store owner if she would allow me to wear a wig through the mall, into the store. From what I hear she was very rude about it and grabbed something out of the back and gave it to them. They brought it out to me and it was an old matted up blonde granny wig.

I made a rash decision that I'd rather go bald than wear that wig. As I walked through the mall to the wig shop, I felt just like I felt in the 4th Grade walking into school wearing that wig. I felt everyone staring at me. Mainly because they were. Everyone was staring at me.

I got to the shop and bought a wig. I bought a red one so at least I left the mall looking fierce! The wig looked beautiful in Denise's wedding. However, Chaz threw a shoe and hit me in the eye a couple of days before the wedding. So, even though my hair was on point – I did have a black eye in all the wedding pictures. I knew better than to let that child watch Austin Powers. As he threw the shoe, he said to me, "I mean honestly, who throws a shoe?" Oh Chaz...

There's a few lessons in this chapter. Obviously, the wig shop owner could have done a better job making me feel comfortable. I get it. Who is to say that we weren't stealing a wig? I get it, but really? No excuse for putting the fear of losing an overpriced (the mark-up was ridiculous) wig over the wellbeing of another human being.

If you own a business, try to make a person's life a little better for having done business with you. There's enough anxiety and stress in our lives to have you add more to it. If nothing else, remember, one day that customer might write a book and tell your story publicly.

BELONGING

One fateful day, a google search on celebrities with Alopecia led an organization called Children's Alopecia Project to me. That's a funny story really. See, because of the Makeover Story episode and me doing some magazine interviews and other television appearances, it became assumed that I was a celebrity.

The funniest instance is my mention in the comments to an article called "10 Celebrities Who Look Better Than Britney Spears Bald." Someone commented to the article that there were celebrities missing from the list and I was named. This is hilarious to me. In fact, I was profiled on several websites, listing me as a celebrity with Alopecia.

I always say, the people who think I am a celebrity have no idea how ordinary I am, and the people who think I'm ordinary have no idea how big of a celebrity I am. It's my own little joke. Again, it makes me laugh.

So these two people, a married couple, with the Children's Alopecia Project (CAP) contacted me and invited me to Philadelphia to speak to a group of children with Alopecia. This was a no-brainer. I instantly said, yes, and I prepared for my trip.

This was huge, I was finally going to meet other people just like me. I was 31 years old and had still never met anyone else with Alopecia.

Come to find out, Jeff and Betsy Woytovich (founders of CAP) created the organization so that their own daughter, Maddie (who has Alopecia) could meet other people just like her. If I have said it once, I've said it a million times, I wish this would have been around when I was growing up. What a difference it would have made in my life.

This was the first year of the CAP event, Alopeciapalooza. I arrived at the hotel, wearing my wig and I saw nothing out of the ordinary.

After checking in, I headed to the elevator to go to my room and freshen up. The elevator stopped and opened and I was met by about 15 bald kids laughing and rushing out the door.

So many emotions and thoughts hit me.

For example:

- Why are they not wearing wigs?

- Why are they all going bald?

- Where are their wigs?

- Is everyone bald?

- Is anyone wearing a wig?

- I hope they don't make me take my wig off!

You get the idea. I went up to my room and after regrouping, I walked down to the area where the event was taking place to check-in with the Woytoviches. Would you believe it, even more bald people? Only this time it was adults. Women, younger and older than me, totally bald. This was insanity. What had I gotten myself into?

After that first day, I went to my room and sat in silence. It's all I could do. I was so overwhelmed by the idea that I wasn't alone and that it was ok to be bald in public that I couldn't breathe. I called my family to tell them how awesome it was and how adorable the kids were. Then I sat in my room and cried.

Throughout the weekend, I would sit through presentations of the other speakers and saw that some of these people were real celebrities. Not fake celebrities like me. I was so intimidated that they wouldn't like me and that they were bald that I didn't even try to get to know any of them.

In fact, Margaret Baker, the co-founder of Women Behaving Baldly (next chapter) was there that weekend and I was too scared to introduce myself to her. Some of people there that weekend have become some of my favorite people in the world and I laugh when I think about how ridiculous I felt around them.

So year one, I wore my wig. Year two, I wore my wig to camp and then took it off during my presentation and kept it in my suitcase during camp. I wore it on the ride and flight back home. Year three, I wore the wig to travel but not at camp. Year four, I travelled bald but packed my wig just in case I needed it. Every year after that, I travelled without the wig altogether. Alopeciapalooza was good for me. I know it was for the kids, but I'm the one who had a breakthrough. Those bald kids are my heroes!

Alopeciapalooza has been going on now for 8 years. I've attended all but one of those camps. I have met what I would describe as family at those events. There's a bald sisterhood that is 6 years strong (remember, I didn't talk to anyone the first year). Ladies like Georgia Van Cuylenburg who does so much good in the world that I can't even begin to say how incredible she is. Kayla Martell, Miss Delaware who taught every little bald girl that she could be bald and be in Miss America! Margaret Baker modelling and breaking the mold of what an actress has to be (aka hairy). Lindsay Walters and Staciana Winfield taking the fitness world by storm proving that this condition is not a handicap.

Now we've added some bald boys to the mix and we've gotten this whole dysfunctional, inappropriate, loving and supportive bald family. Alopecia is not like other conditions. We are all world changers. It's as if when the hair fell out, something even better (heroism maybe?) took its place. You can name just about any famous Alopecian and I've either met them, know them or call them a personal friend. What other condition does that?

How many people with Parkinson's Disease knows Michael J. Fox personally? How many people with Cancer can call Hugh Jackman up on their cell phone and say hello? This is an extraordinary group of people that see the need for community. Alopecians are awesome! We are literally taking over the world.

One of my favorite stories was something that happened in a Cheesecake Factory Restaurant in Charlotte, NC. Our waiter was bald and he asked me how I got my head in such a close shave. I explained that I had Alopecia and he said, "Oh wow! Do you know Kevin Bull?" Here's what's funny, Kevin Bull is from American Ninja Warrior fame. Anyone that watches that show knows of him and roots for him. He's a great guy. He's also a CAP Mentor. I am a CAP Mentor. Again, in a normal community, my answer would have been no. BUT not in Alopecia World!

"Yes, I do know Kevin Bull. He's awesome."

That's how I ended up with such a fantastic individual contributing to my book's foreword. We are an awesome little community that takes care of each other. Anthony Carrigan (Gotham, The Flash, Blacklist, Parenthood) has created a movement among Alopecians referring to us as Unicorns. It stuck. Now we are an awesome unicorn community. Watch out, we are taking over the world. It's a little weird, but we're bald, so get over it.

The coolest part about all of this is watching the children of CAP grow. I see them go through a similar transition as I did. They start out shy trying to cover up their bald heads but as they get comfortable in their own skin with the encouragement of their new bald friends, they just blossom. Each year they add more and more participation to the event involving the CAP kids. The past several years they've had kids sit on a panel. Now that some of the children are growing up and going to college, they are coming back to speak and be CAP

Mentors. The future of our community is in good hands.

That's your lesson this chapter: Find community. After Denise shaved her head in support of me (you're going to love that story), she went with me to an Alopeciapalooza Camp and we shared our story. After we finished speaking, so many parents came to me with tears in their eyes wishing their child had a "Denise." Find your people. Find your Denise. That person or group of people that get you and that you can relate to.

Find your forever friend and hold on to that person. How does that change the world? Sometimes you make decisions or discoveries that change the world as a whole but sometimes it just changes your world. Anything that makes you a better person will in the long run make the world a better place.

PEOPLE

As I grew into adulthood, my alopecia developed into what is called Alopecia Universalis. Basically, bald universally. That means that it's a little more obvious and "freaky" because I do not have eyelashes, eyebrows and all that.

Sometimes people compliment me and sometimes they offend me. I've been driven to tears by the thoughtless words of another person. I have been moved to tears by the kind words from others. There is something about being a bald woman in society that makes strangers think that they have an open invitation for an inappropriate discussion.

This phenomenon birthed an idea between me and fellow Alopecian, Margaret Baker. One night during Camp, we got to laughing at all of the things that people have said and done over the years. Margaret and I stayed awake long after everyone else fell asleep and she mentioned that we need to do something creative with these stories.

The next morning, I cornered her in the hallway and said, "Women Behaving Baldly!" I remember lots of giggling, lots of hugs and glances of "this is awesome" between us after that. We knew we were on to something. After interviewing women from all over the world, that gut feeling was confirmed. After announcing Women Behaving Baldly, we knew we needed something more G Rated for the girls so we created Little Women Behaving Baldly. This is a project that we are still working together on today.

One of our most popular things we get told is, "you are so lucky!" I'm not kidding. Constantly I'm told how lucky I am that I don't have to fix my hair, shave my legs or even just that someone thinks it's hard to have curly hair. I have to remind myself to show empathy because I really want to reply with, "you're so right, I'd much rather not have to shave my legs than have hair!"

Not every stranger approaching me is a negative one. My Dad had to have a medical procedure done and my brother and I met up at the hospital to wait with Mom. After having dinner in the cafeteria, I ran into the restroom for a quick potty break. As I was washing my hands, a little girl around five years old was staring at me. "Are you a girl, this is the girl's bathroom?" she asked. I told her that I was in fact a girl and she questioned me being bald. I heard her mother's voice come out from one of the stalls, "I am so sorry."

I continued to talk to her and I explained that I had Alopecia, an autoimmune disease and that my body couldn't grow hair. She responded with, "oh yeah, I have a friend that has something like that, she has hair down to her butt." I laughed and said, "yep, exactly the same thing." From under the bathroom stall, her mother repeated, "I am so sorry."

I thanked the little girl for asking me about my hair and thanked the mother for letting me talk to her about it. Some of my best interactions have been as a result of an inquisitive child.

The best way I've ever heard my situation explained was at a Fresh Market grocery store. A little girl, around the same age as the one I just told you about, asked her mother why the woman behind them (me) was bald. Her mother's response was, "some people have brown hair, some people have blonde hair, and some people have no hair at all. That lady has no hair." The little girl accepted the answer and they went about their day.

I was sincerely moved by that explanation. It was the first time that I felt like a normal human being. There was no sickness or deformity associated with my situation. For the first time, it felt like I had made a choice to be bald and that it was a socially acceptable decision. That mother and her little girl empowered me more in that one conversation than almost anyone else has (second only to Cross telling me my hair was beautiful).

As I was travelling with a friend, she was complaining that she always gets stopped and patted down by TSA. I knew that my license could be an issue because I was bald in person but wearing a wig on my license. As I approached the license check, the agent spent a little longer looking at my identification than normal. I grew concerned.

He handed me my ID back and I began to walk away. "Ma'am," he stopped me. My heart stopped and I worried that he was going to question my identification. My friend raised her eyebrows thinking the same. I turned to him and he said to me, "you are beautiful with or without hair." I thanked him and walked away. My friend laughed until she got pulled over for her pat down.

I've had so many fun situations on airplanes. I have a back issue and boarding a plane after it has started filling up often times bothers my back. I've learned to ask for early boarding so I do not have back pain the entire flight.

When I would attempt to board early wearing a wig, the flight attendants would give me a skeptical look, as if to say, "whatever." If I am bald when I try to board early, that doesn't happen. I've always found it so funny. When my friends travelling with me benefit from this early boarding "Alopecia Perk," they love me.

Once while flying back from New York City, I had a drunk couple sitting behind me. They had been discussing me quite loudly and as they spoke of me, I kept notes of what they were saying on a legal pad. My favorite part of the conversation was when the husband told the wife that I must be a lawyer. When she asked how we knew, he replied, "she's writing on a legal pad so she must be a lawyer." The wife dubbed me, "The Bald Lawyer." Not longer after that statement, they both passed out.

Another flight mishap happened when I was seated next to the cutest college guy on a packed plane. He was travelling with a group of friends and they were all seated in different areas of the plane. As his girlfriend walked by and saw him sitting beside me chatting it up, she gave me such an evil look. In fact, as we traveled, I would look back at her and the death stare continued the whole flight. It was at that moment that I thought up the t-shirt idea of, "Don't You Wish Your Girlfriend Was Bald Like Me?" Well, don't you?

I've learned to hold on and be inspired by the humorous and to disconnect from the negative. I smile and laugh daily and I try to create the same life moments in those I interact with. To state the obvious, emotions are contagious. Spread joy so that you are surrounded by happiness.

Bad days happen and negatives people come and go, but the moments that make you smile can last a lifetime in your memories. Let them.

Be the reason for the smile on someone's face.

FREE

Have you ever worn a wig? They are tight (or too loose), itchy and most of the time uncomfortable. I was always aware of the fact that I had on a wig. I would sit and think, "I am wearing a wig."

For years I had wanted to abandon the wig and live life as a bald woman. I had not received much encouragement from some influential people in my life. I was warned that going bald would be professional suicide. The warning was that my job and our clients would judge me and it would prevent me from being taken seriously.

One Sunday morning I was in church, when a bald man walked by my row. I nudged the person beside me and said, "Can you believe that man is coming to church bald? He should cover that up!"

The rest of the service, I sat there furious that I had to have a wig on. I recognized that I was beginning to get bitter. I knew that something had to give.

I had discussed coming out bald to family and friends many times. It was even an argument between some of us at this point. There was even a suggestion made that me going bald full time was an attempt for attention.

It was argued by some that my husband had dated and married a woman who wore a wig and was beautiful. Being bald was sickly. Would my husband even want to be married to a bald woman? If not, I didn't know if I wanted to be married to someone who was not willing to let me live my life free.

So I did what any Marketer worthy her salt would do, I bought a domain name and became the Bald Marketer. This new way of life happened slow at first and then fast like a bullet.

One of the girls on my team at work, Tera, was also a photographer. I asked her if she would take a fun picture of me one day during work.

We picked a day and I got all made up and we went into one of the studio rooms and we took an epic photo.

In this photo, I am standing there bald, holding my wig. In another photo, I am throwing the wig behind me. It felt so liberating. Tera made me look fantastic, as she always does. I knew the time had come.

I was at a point where regardless of how it made other people feel, I had no choice. I had to live my life in a way that made me happy. In the instance of my husband, he had a choice. He could choose to stay married to a bald woman or he could leave. I didn't give him an ultimatum by any means, but as a grown man, he had a choice. He made the right choice.

At the time, I was the Marketing Director for a Production Company in Charlotte, NC. Not too bad for a high school drop-out if I do say so myself. Anyway, I wanted to make sure there wasn't an issue with me being bald at work. Here's the thing, legally, they couldn't tell me no. I could sue them. However, I did want my superiors to know that I respected their dress code and wouldn't do anything so major without their blessing.

After leaving work on a Friday and taking my wig off in the car on the way home, I made the decision that I would no longer wear a wig to work. I'd had this thought many times over the years and had even had employers discourage it.

This was the email and how it all went down:

I'm really struggling with the ok-ness of being a bald professional. Honestly – I think it's a branding element of me that's cool. I thought about starting the bald pro Laura on Monday. Your thoughts?

(I'm just really sick of the wigs – lol)

Laura Hudson
Marketing Director

Their response was a resounding YES! In fact, to quote them – they said:

CEO: I have always been completely fine with a bald Laura in the office. If you are ready... We are ready.

COO: I say go ahead... It's a natural part of being you...

HR: We accept you for who you are; wigs make no difference.

So that next Monday marked my first day at work bald. The entire staff was beyond supportive. No strange looks... No awkward comments... In fact, it was like nothing had changed. They even told me how much they thought it added to the environment.

As the first year living wig free passed, the influential members of the negative crowd saw the impact of this freedom on both me and the public. It didn't hinder me and it looked good on me. Sometimes you have to stand up for what is right and wait for the naysayers to see how much the yay outweighs their nay.

I was confident in my decision to go bald publicly or come out bald as we refer to it. However, occasionally doubt would creep in. I would worry that I was embarrassing my kids. I worried that no one would want to date me because they either thought I was sick or hideous. For some reason, being bald made me feel fat. I know that makes no sense, but it really did.

One day as Lyv and I were walking towards our apartment, I asked her if I embarrassed her. She told me that I did not. I tried to make her feel comfortable with honesty, hoping she wasn't just trying to spare my feelings.

I asked her more specifically, is it easier to have a Mom that wears a wig than one that is bald? She told me that I looked great bald. In fact, I'll quote her. She said, "You look so much prettier bald than you do in a bad wig."

You know what? She was right.

I felt prettier bald than I did in a bad wig. The whole being aware of the wig feeling completely vanished when I came out bald. Obviously, it made sense that it would. The only problem is that I was so comfortable bald that I often forgot I was, well, bald. When I meet new people or speak at a non-Alopecia event, often times I forget to tell them why I am bald. I feel so normal. Let me add here, I can't wait for the day that the rest of the world sees me as normal and doesn't require an explanation.

I've been asked, "What if a job required me to wear a wig?" It would depend on the job! If my job is starring in a blockbuster film, then yeah, I'm selling out and wearing a wig. This is one of those "case by case basis" scenarios. I'm as much of a bald activist as you can get but I'm not stupid.

When I felt it was time to move on professionally from the Production Company, I had to decide if I was going to go through the interview process bald or with the wig. I chose to not take a step back and continue interviewing bald. It didn't hinder me at all. In fact, I think it set me apart from the other job candidates.

In 2015, I attended a marketing event in Boston, Massachusetts called Inbound. It was a marketing nerd's dream come true!

I would tweet during the event as the Bald Marketer and started getting a little attention with my branding. Compliments were being tweeted to me and even folks wondering if I was a speaker rather than just an attendee. (There's a not so subtle hint to the folks at Inbound. See what I did there?)

There was a movement that had happened that I was so interested in. The "It Was Never a Dress" movement. It was this photo of the Women's Restroom signed recolored to show that she was wearing a cape and not a skirt. Margaret and I had both always wanted to meet the people behind this image because we thought it was so profound and aligned with what we were doing with Women Behaving Baldly.

One day, during Inbound 2015, a lady walked up to me and complimented me for my boldness. She said she had seen me and knew she had to meet me. We stood and talked for a moment and exchanged hairloss stories and business cards.

Then she handed me a sticker, and that's when I found out that who I had just met was Tania Katan. Tania was one of the creators behind It Was Never a Dress. Another win for being bald!

Seeing all the good things that have come from me embracing being bald reminds me of a Mentor in my life, Pastor Robert Frazier. Back when I wore a wig regularly, he asked me to tell my story for church one Sunday night, and he thought it would be awesome if I ripped off my wig and told it bald. I laughed at him and declined the suggestion.

He would say that to me all the time. He would tell me it would be so cool if I would do my speeches bald. Just like EE, I think that if he were alive and could see me now, he would say to me, "I told you so. Can I say that?"

Yet another person sent into my life, trying to make me great that I ignored and even laughed off their suggestion. Is that what you are doing? Are you constantly turning a deaf ear to people trying to make you great?

Don't take any moment for granted. When you meet someone who can invest in your wellbeing, open up to them and let them. Listen to what they have to say. See yourself through their eyes. If they think you can be a world changer, listen and consider taking that path.

A world changer knows that no one you meet is an accident. They either represent something you should be or something you should avoid. Let to know the difference.

LOVED

Being a woman who lives her life publicly bald, I am constantly explaining myself. I have to explain to perfect strangers why I am bald and to people that I am close to why I choose to not cover up my bald head with a hat or a wig. I can't say I'm ever lonely.

There's always someone with an opinion, story or question.

I prefer it though. I live by the philosophy that if I didn't want to have to talk about being bald, I should cover it up. When you take a bold stand and do something so radical, such as going against the grain as I have, you have to be prepared for the stares and commentary.

Here's my point of view though: If you have the time to stop and question me about being bald, you have the time to hear my story.

Case in point, I once had a lady stop me at the YMCA and ask me if I was wearing a wig. A very rude question we established at this point right? So I told her. For 20 minutes, I told her about Alopecia and growing up different.

The next day, a friend of hers mentioned it to me in the childcare room. She said to me that the friend had complained that she asked me a simple question and I went on for 20 minutes about my life story. I laughed and said to her, "Yes I did. I figured if she was rude enough to ask me if I was wearing a wig, I could be rude and take up 20 minutes of her precious time explaining why. Now she knows." Needless to say, we didn't have Mommy/Daughter play dates as a result of it but I made my point.

As many instances of awkwardness that I've had to face, there's been an equal and overwhelming number of instances of love. One such instance was in 2014.

On July 4, 2014, Denise Mullis sacrificed a great deal for me. We had been best friends for nearly 30 years and she had bit her tongue and hid her frustrations long enough!

Denise walked the hallways with me at school a
I was teased and tormented by classmates. She
heard the laughs and jokes about my wig even
when I didn't.

The sacrifice she made nearly 30 years later?

Denise shaved her head to see what it would be
like to live as a bald woman.

These are a few of her journal entries.

My life as a bald woman, Day 1:

> Loved this day! So happy I was able to
> share this experience with Laura. It was a
> very emotional day. Didn't realize how
> prickly my head was going to feel! I find
> myself thinking about how Laura deals
> with looks and stares on a daily basis.

My life as a bald woman, Day 2:

> I didn't realize how drafty our house is!

> I can feel the air from the ceiling fan onto
> my head. Some stares from folk in the
> grocery store. Some smiles and
> sympathetic looks. Others just appear to
> be treating me as they would anybody
> else, which I find comforting.

Have ran into several people who know me, but didn't know about the fundraiser; they thought I had cancer and were concerned, so I explained.

My life as a bald woman, Day 3:

Impacting my family more than me. I feel comfortable with my decision, but am realizing my family is being affected and impacted as well. We tend to be an introverted family, so the extra attention from others is feeling a little uncomfortable for them at times.

There are no more journal entries because it was more overwhelming than she thought it would be. It was more painful than she could put into words. The thoughtless words of others and judgment she received was more than expected. She became more self aware of her physical flaws (her words) because she couldn't hide behind her hair.

When I told my parents that I was planning to come out bald, my Mom cried. She asked me if I was sure. When I said I was and why I was, she told me she was proud of me. The first few times I went out bald, I could see tears in her eyes sometimes.

I don't know if she cried because she was so proud or because she was afraid I would get hurt. I like to think she cried because she knew that together, we had beaten the odds.

Remember the doctors telling them to get used to a bald kid? How we didn't know what that meant? Now they know. Having a bald kid means that you've got this bold, brave, self confident, sometimes arrogant but beautiful child that is destined to change the world. It took more than 30 years to find out what that meant but here we are now, finally with an answer.

The people that love you, like my family and Denise, will be there for you in pain or celebration. They will help you figure out how to navigate the changes in your life so that you come out on the right side of happy. When other people around you are just strangers pointing and whispering, your people are there ready to take a razor to their head and look just like you, metaphorically speaking of course.

Had I let the fear of what people might say or might do decide my fate, I would have never come out bald. Not everyone in my life came through for me but the ones that did came through in a big way. They showed up.

That's my advice here. Be you and do so with boldness. Close your eyes and ears to the ones that can't handle it. At the same time, keep your eyes and ears open for the ones that rise up and become great right along with you. It might be an unlikely friend or family member but these will be your people.

They will be the unlikely compliment to your efforts to change the world. You won't be able to do it without them. They wouldn't be involved without you. As you are made stronger, they will be as well.

We're just a bunch of unicorn world changers begetting more unicorn world changers. Let's do this!

CURSED

One of the most hurtful things ever said to me happened in 2016, nearly 2 years after coming out bald. I had been raised in church and had a strong faith in the Christian God myself. I learned a long time ago, and it's even more true now than ever, don't judge God on God's followers.

This story is the case study for that statement. I hesitated to put it in the book because the bad stories are the ones that always make the headlines. The church doesn't need one more story of stupidity. Unfortunately, I have a story myself. I decided to include it because it matters and I owe it to my Dad to make sure nobody's ever made to feel like he was years ago.

I was visiting a church with my family and a lady sat down beside me and asked if I had cancer.

I get that question a lot and it does irritate me, but I've learned to answer gracefully, as I did this day. She then admitted to me that her husband had Alopecia and that if he would just not stress out so much his hair would come back. She was really testing my patience.

I tried to see myself as a source of support and education for her. I offered to speak to her husband and sit down with them and tell them what I know about Alopecia. First thing being, stress-free life is not the cure. She kept rattling on about how horrible it was. Then she told me that she was going to pray that God would heal me. I thanked her and said, I prayed that everyday for years. I'm ok with not being healed because I think God has allowed me to carry this to make a difference in the lives of others. I'm ok with the me He created.

What happened next took me by surprise so quickly that I'm surprised I didn't cuss in church. She became legitimately angry and told me, "I'm going to have to stop you right there. I rebuke you. My God is not a God of sickness. This disease is a curse and you should not blame God for it." She specifically referred to it as a curse in my bloodline.

She went on to talk about sin in my parents' life and how Alopecia was a curse that needed to be broken. She even said she didn't know why her husband had been cursed, maybe for being so stressed. WHAT?

I got a little red in the face and told her that I would actually pray for her. She was the one cursed. I said, "Let's define the curse - is me having Alopecia and living my life completely bald the curse or is your need to be defined by beautiful hair and not being able to see me as normal the curse?"

We sat next to each other. She looked ahead and I looked at her. She got up and sat a few rows ahead of me and I fumed the rest of the service. I ended up leaving early and never went back.

I'm so glad she said that to me, someone who could separate human from spiritual. Had she said this to someone else, the ending could have been much different. Take a lesson from this story, don't enforce your perceptions on another person, especially if that person is facing a difficult situation.

It's so hard to move forward and use your difference when you are having to view yourself through the perception of others. When you look around at your circumstances, it's easy to drown in them. They are suffocating. I am so grateful that years ago, when I got to the point that I couldn't change the way the world saw me, I decided to change the way I saw the world.

Living in your true purpose means living beyond the perception of your circumstances. Your circumstances are what you see on the surface. Often times, they are temporary pain. In the beginning of the book I mentioned having a car repossessed. That's a temporary pain and, man, for a little while it hurts. It feels hopeless and you don't see how you can move on from it.

You do move on. You do live to see another day. You go from one day to the next and then one day it's over.

The same is true for losing your hair. It might feel like a curse at first. The first day turns into years of mourning. You have to let it go. You have to accept it because you can't change it. The advice I always give to people when they lose their hair is, "mourn today, dance tomorrow."

I always joke that it would be funny if after all of these years of being bald, my hair came back when I was 70 years old, white as snow. One of the most common things people say to me is, "at least you'll never go grey!" I think it would be quite ironic (even Alanis Morissette ironic) if my hair came back that way. I really would have to simply laugh at that one. That, in fact, might be the curse. Who knows?

If my hair came back, I would be happy but also as my story changed my mission in life would change.

Another question I get is, if there is a cure would I take it. I would need you to define the word "cure" in order to answer this question.

Many drugs carry side effects that in my opinion are so much worse than being bald. I'm not willing to trade one issue for another. If it was discovered that a certain dietary lifestyle was the cure, such as veganism or vegetarianism, I would go for it.

If it worked, I would, however, have to get creative and come up with something as unique as The Bald Marketer - The Once Bald Marketer maybe?

ENOUGH

Be you, you rock. That phrase is my autograph.
I've signed books, t-shirts, arms and bald
heads. I needed something that set me apart
from all of the other autographs. I'm a marketer
after all. It needed to be good! On a whim while
signing a super cool bald kid's book, I wrote, "Be
You - You Rock!" I liked it. It sounded like
something I'd say and is easy to sign as an
autograph. So what does it mean?

If you are going to change the world, you must
start by changing your world. Find the self-
confidence within you to acknowledge that you
are awesome just as you are.

Once you've changed your own world and
accepted the fact that you do indeed rock,
expand your reach and spread that virus to
those around you.

This leads us to the last lesson of this book. If you really want to be a world changer, you've got to learn to accept who you are, how you look or what makes you different. When you accept you, it makes it so much easier to accept others. Everyone has something that makes them different. That's the only thing that makes us all the same.

There's absolutely nothing that you could do that would make you any less worthy of greatness than everybody else on this planet.

You are in control. You are driving this car!

Here's the thing. Some things in your life are simply out of your control. There is absolutely nothing you can do to change those things.

You've got two choices:

1. Let it ruin you.

2. Let it make you.

Had I listened to my hurts back in High School and given them control, I wouldn't be here today. I would have never survived that hurt.

It doesn't matter that I'm bald. It doesn't matter that I don't look like you. I might matter to everyone else, but the day I decided that their opinion no longer mattered to me was the day I felt truly free.

I spent so many years constantly aware that I was wearing a wig. I would sit in class or church or at work and feel it on my head. It felt like a tumor that didn't belong on my body. It bothered me more than anyone knew. I was so self conscious that everyone was looking at me, talking about me and laughing at me. In my mind, everyone was laughing at me.

After a few months of living free, bald, without the wig, I gained this freedom that I can't even explain. Now when people stare at me or laugh at me, I don't even care. I know it's because I'm bald. I also know it makes them jerks. If they are laughing at me, they are just bad people. I don't have to answer for them. I'm free, they are not.

That's what I want for you.

What is it you need to break free from? There is no addiction, suppression, depression or condition that you can't shake. It may be hard. It may require every ounce of strength and will you have within you.

Muster it up within you and don't believe for one minute that you are anything less than a story that needs to be heard, a life that wants to be changed and a gift that must be shared.

You've finished this book. You've got a few good tools in your chest to make a difference in the world around you. Go change the world. When you do, send me an email and tell me about it.

Email me at laura@worldchangersguide.com

The end. World Changed.

ABOUT THE AUTHOR

Since childhood, Laura has been completely bald. Her hair loss is as a result of Alopecia Universalis, an auto-immune condition for which there is no cure. Growing up, Laura was constantly teased and tormented at school, had few friends and was told that she would never amount to very much. Fearing rejection, she hid the fact that she wore a wig for fifteen years, even as an adult. Not anymore!

She made the decision to boldly embrace her difference and created her entire branding around it. Laura Hudson, the Bald Marketer, is the co-creator of Women Behaving Baldly and an advocate for the Children's Alopecia Project.

In addition to working full-time in the Marketing Industry, she travels performing speaking engagements incorporating both life and comedy into her events.

Laura has three children and lives in Fort Mill, SC.

More Information:

For information on this book or to book Laura Hudson as a speaker at your event, visit her online at:

www.WorldChangersGuide.com
www.BaldMarketer.com

Email her at laura@worldchangersguide.com.

Facebook:

https://www.facebook.com/worldchangersguide/
https://www.facebook.com/BaldMarketer/
https://www.facebook.com/WomenBehavingBaldly/

Twitter: @lauracarrhudson

Instagram: @lauracarrhudson

For more information or to donate to the **Children's Alopecia Project**, visit them online at https://childrensalopeciaproject.org.

Made in the USA
Columbia, SC
01 August 2018